GOAT BOY

Lou Kuenzler

Illustrated by Phil Corbett

The EDGE Crew

Isabel Thomas

OXFORD
UNIVERSITY PRESS

Great Clarendon Street, Oxford, OX2 6DP, United Kingdom

Oxford University Press is a department of the University of Oxford. It furthers the University's objective of excellence in research, scholarship, and education by publishing worldwide. Oxford is a registered trade mark of Oxford University Press in the UK and in certain other countries.

Text © Oxford University Press 2025

Illustrations © Phil Corbett 2025

The moral rights of the author have been asserted

First published in 2025

All rights reserved. No part of this publication may be reproduced, stored in a retrieval system, transmitted, used for text and data mining, or used for training artificial intelligence, in any form or by any means, without the prior permission in writing of Oxford University Press, or as expressly permitted by law, by licence or under terms agreed with the appropriate reprographics rights organization. Enquiries concerning reproduction outside the scope of the above should be sent to the Rights Department, Oxford University Press, at the address above.

You must not circulate this work in any other form and you must impose this same condition on any acquirer

British Library Cataloguing in Publication Data

Data available

ISBN: 978-1-382-05309-9

10 9 8 7 6 5 4 3 2 1

The manufacturing process conforms to the environmental regulations of the country of origin.

Printed in China by Golden Cup

Acknowledgements

Goat Boy written by Lou Kuenzler; *The EDGE Crew* written by Isabel Thomas

The publisher and authors would like to thank the following for permissions to use copyright material:
Front cover: Phil Corbett
Back Cover: Nature Picture Library / Alamy Stock Photo; All Canada Photos / Alamy Stock Photo; JENYA / Alamy Stock Photo; Danita Delimont / Alamy Stock Photo.

Photos: p19(a): SJ Travel Photo and Video / Shutterstock; p19(b): Cookie Studio / Shutterstock; p19(c): Asier Romero / Shutterstock; p19(d): Gerald Corsi / E+ / Getty Images; pp20-21(a): blickwinkel / Alamy Stock Photo; pp20-21(b): GFC Collection / Alamy Stock Photo; pp20-21(c): Nature Picture Library / Alamy Stock Photo; pp20-21(d): Danny Ye / Shutterstock; pp20-21(e): All Canada Photos / Alamy Stock Photo; pp20-21(f): Zoonar GmbH / Alamy Stock Photo; pp20-21(g): mike lane / Alamy Stock Photo; pp20-21(h): Fernando Romão / Alamy Stock Photo; pp20-21(i): jack perks / Alamy Stock Photo; pp20-21(j): JENYA / Alamy Stock Photo; pp20-21(k): Minden Pictures / Alamy Stock Photo; pp20-21(l): Nature Picture Library / Alamy Stock Photo; pp20-21(m): Holm94 / Shutterstock; p22: Nature Picture Library / Alamy Stock Photo; p23: K JAYARAM / SCIENCE PHOTO LIBRARY; p24: All Canada Photos / Alamy Stock Photo; p25: KEVIN ELSBY / Alamy Stock Photo; p26: JENYA / Alamy Stock Photo; p27: Matthijs Kuijpers / Alamy Stock Photo; p28(t): GFC Collection / Alamy Stock Photo; p28(b): Marcin Mierzejewski / Shutterstock; p29(t): Jenny Matthews / Alamy Stock Photo; p29(b): Danita Delimont / Alamy Stock Photo; p30(l): Fernando Romão / Alamy Stock Photo; p30(tr): Holm94 / Shutterstock; p30(br): mike lane / Alamy Stock Photo; p31(l): Zoonar GmbH / Alamy Stock Photo; p31(r): jack perks / Alamy Stock Photo; p32(l): All Canada Photos / Alamy Stock Photo; p32(ml): GFC Collection / Alamy Stock Photo; p32(mr): Nature Picture Library / Alamy Stock Photo; p32(r): JENYA / Alamy Stock Photo.

Every effort has been made to contact copyright holders of material reproduced in this book. Any omissions will be rectified in subsequent printings if notice is given to the publisher.

Contents

Goat Boy   5

The EDGE Crew   19

Green words

Single-syllable words

grown boat toast

Multi-syllabic words

Oak|wood o|pen gold|en co|rri|dor
note|book

Root words and suffixes

change → changing   happy → happily
notice → notices   approach → approaches

Red words

come here everyone other any

Challenge words

shy head beard new though wolf

GOAT BOY

Billy is the new kid at school. He feels shy.

Billy slips into the changing rooms. When he looks in the mirror he gasps in shock.

Two golden yellow horns have grown from the crown of his head. He has a little beard, too.

The door swings open. A PE teacher and a load of boys pile in.

Billy pulls up his hood.

Billy and Hasan go across the playground to the art room.

It's hot and stuffy in the art room.

"Coat off in here!" says the teacher, Ms Oakwood. "If you get paint on it, you will have to soak it for days."

Billy takes his coat off. He notices that everyone has a quick peek at the horns on his head. But nobody says anything.

Hasan smiles at him.

"Welcome to art class!" says Ms Oakwood, with a gentle nod.

"Sorry Miss!"

"No problem."

Billy eats his notebook.

munch! munch!

Being a goat makes him *very* hungry.

He eats a painting of a boat.

I'm still hungry!

chomp chomp

Stop! I will *not* have a goat in my class if you're going to eat the art!

Ms Oakwood gives him a box to munch.

crunch!
munch!

"Nobody has pointed at me or been mean, even though I turned into a goat," Billy tells Hasan as they get their coats.

"You'll change back when you settle in. A goat is nothing!" Hasan grins. "A new boy last week turned into a wolf. He ate a teacher!"

"Oh!" says Billy. He happily munches his coat.

I don't feel so shy anymore.

Green words

Single-syllable words

crew   shrew   hear   true

Multi-syllabic words

dis|app|ear   chem|i|cals   ex|tinct   sur|vive
in|cred|i|ble   re|prod|uce

Root words and suffixes

renew → renewed   protect → protecting
evolve → evolved   stole → stolen

Red words

people   love   by   water   talk

Challenge words

endangered   aye-aye   vulture
Bechstein's   great

The EDGE Crew

ONE-YEAR-OLD PANDA APPEARS ON LIVE FEED

 Seen the news? Too cute!

 I'm going to do something to help these animals.

FUNDING RENEWED FOR SEA OTTER ZOO!

 But not all animals in need of help look cute.

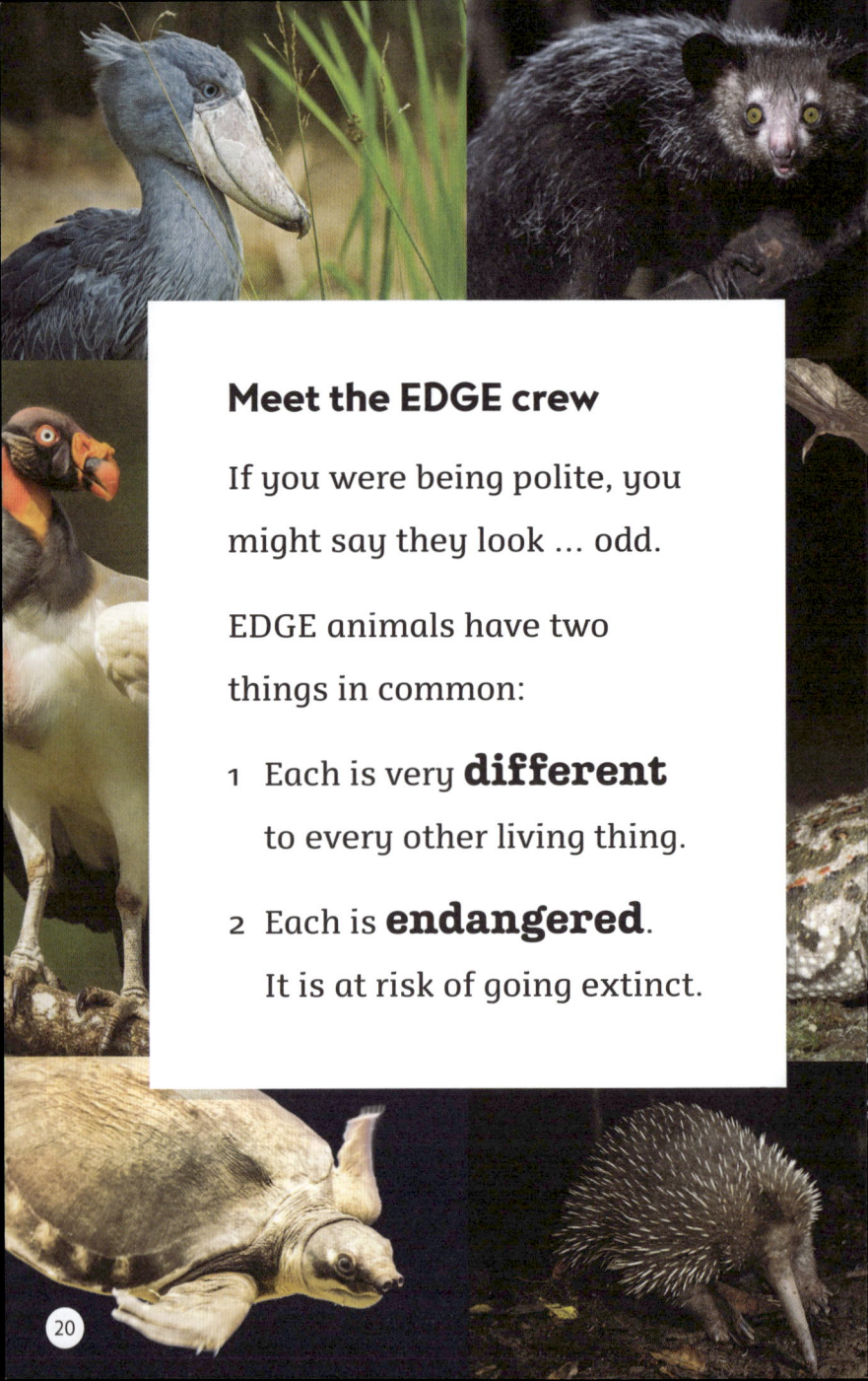

Meet the EDGE crew

If you were being polite, you might say they look ... odd.

EDGE animals have two things in common:

1 Each is very **different** to every other living thing.

2 Each is **endangered**. It is at risk of going extinct.

The EDGE crew need our help just as much as cute animals do.

Without our help, these rare beasts may disappear forever.

- So what can I do?
- Tell people about them!
- I don't even know their names.
- I'm getting to that …

1 Purple frog

- muffin-sized
- bloated body
- short legs

 It looks like it came from my nose.

 Yes. But I love that such odd animals exist!

Over time, purple frogs evolved to be better at hiding. This helped them to survive. Today, they spend most of their time in **burrows**. This keeps them safe from other animals, but not from people. Sadly, purple frogs are hunted for food. Their forest habitats are being cut down, too.

To see where the purple frog and other EDGE animals live, look at page 32.

2 King vulture

- eats from carcasses
- bare skin gets smeared with goo
- lives alone or in pairs (rare for vultures)
- likes to do cartwheels to impress mates

These birds are not known for their good looks.

Despite their **disgusting** manners, these birds do an important job. They clear up when something dies.

Today, few king vultures are seen. Experts fear they are being harmed by chemicals from farms.

Eating rotting meat. Yuck.

It's grim to us, but they love it!

3 Pitted-shelled turtle

- webbed feet
- skin-coated shell
- large nostrils

This incredible turtle evolved to be different to all other turtles.

 Its nose looks like a plug socket!

 Yes, it looks very different to other turtles that live in fresh water.

People take these turtles from rivers and smuggle them to be kept as pets. Even their eggs are **stolen**.

This makes it hard for the turtles to reproduce. It takes 16 years for a turtle to lay its first egg.

4 Aye-aye (say: igh-igh)

- teeth never stop growing
- large ears
- long middle finger to dig grubs from bark

Most lemurs look cute and cuddly. The aye-aye is different.

ring-tailed lemur

Aye-ayes are at risk. The **forests** where they live are being cleared for farming.

Some people think that aye-ayes bring bad luck. They are even killed for this reason.

 Why would people think that aye-ayes are unlucky?

They hear tales that are not true.

It's not just cute animals that need protecting. Not-so-cute animals are endangered, too.

This includes animals that might live near **you** ...

* **Adder**

* **Natterjack toad**

* **Water shrew**

So if I want to help EDGE animals, what do I do?

 Talk about them! If more people knew these odd animals exist, they would want to help, too!

Bechstein's bat

* **Great crested newt**

 I've found a website with more facts about EDGE animals:
https://www.edgeofexistence.org

Glossary

Goat Boy

approaches: comes nearer to someone

crown: the top of someone's head

lie low: avoid being noticed by people

transforming: changing in a big way

The EDGE Crew

carcass: a dead animal

EDGE species: this stands for 'Evolutionarily Distinct and Globally Endangered' species

fresh water: water that is not sea water

habitats: places where animals live in the wild

renewed: repeated so it keeps going

smeared: covered